We're Going on a Bear Hunt

LET'S DISCOVER
BIRDS

This book belongs to:

. . . .

WALKER
ENTERTAINMENT

First published 2018 by Walker Entertainment
an imprint of Walker Books Ltd
87 Vauxhall Walk, London SE11 5HJ

2 4 6 8 10 9 7 5 3 1

© 2016 Bear Hunt Films Ltd
Text by Andrea Cascardi/Walker Books Ltd

Based on the animated film developed and produced by Lupus Films in
association with Bear Hunt Films and Walker Productions for Channel 4,
Universal Pictures and Herrick Entertainment with the support of
Creative Europe – MEDIA programme of the European Union.
Licensed by Walker Productions Ltd.

Created in consultation with Michael Rosen and Helen Oxenbury

Additional wildlife illustrations by Mat Williams/Bear Hunt Films Ltd
Line art by Susanna Chapman

This book has been typeset in Plantin Infant and Dina's Handwriting

Printed in China

British Library Cataloguing in Publication Data:
a catalogue record for this book is available from the British Library

ISBN 978-1-4063-7995-2
www.walker.co.uk

All recipes are for informational and/or entertainment purposes only;
please check ingredients carefully if you have any allergies and,
if in doubt, consult a health professional.

Let's get going!

Birds are amazing creatures and you can find them almost anywhere! Whether you want to look at them in your garden or go exploring further afield, this great guide will help you learn about the birds you discover along the way.

Activity

If you spot any birds that aren't in this book, sketch them in a journal and find out about them when you get home.

Stay safe

Exploring is fun, but it's important to follow these simple dos and don'ts to stay safe:

- Always explore with an adult.

- Take care when crossing roads.

- Don't touch any plants or creatures unless you know it is safe to do so.

Plan your bird adventure!

Before you start your adventure, use this list to think about what to take on your bird search.

Sticker activity 🐾
Colour in your four item stickers and stick them in the boxes below.

You might want to pack:
- suncream
- a hat
- water
- plasters
- antiseptic cream

If it's cold, you could take:
- a warm hat
- a scarf
- gloves
- warm socks

If it's wet outside, you may want:
- wellies and a rain hat
- a poncho or raincoat
- an umbrella

Other equipment:
- a camera
- a journal
- a magnifying glass

Habitat is the natural home of a living thing.

How to find birds

Bird-watching requires two things:
patience and observation.

Try not to make loud noises and never disturb a bird's **habitat** – this way you'll make sure they keep returning.

Birds Close to Home

Fun fact
*Birds shed their feathers
at least once a year.*

Homebirds

You don't have to travel very far from home to discover lots of amazing birds.

What is a bird?

Birds are **vertebrate** animals that have two feet, feathers and wings.

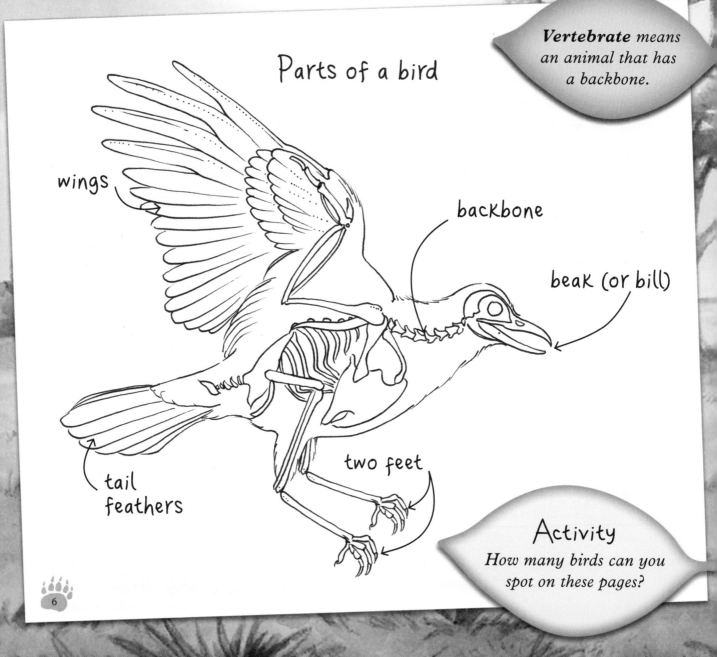

Parts of a bird

wings

backbone

beak (or bill)

tail feathers

two feet

Vertebrate means an animal that has a backbone.

Activity
How many birds can you spot on these pages?

Know before you go

Going on a bird search will be much more fun once you know these important bird facts.

Appearance

Male and female birds of the same **species** can look very different.

Flight

Some birds have hollow bones, which make them light enough to fly.

Migration

Most birds move around the world depending on the weather.

Moulting

Birds shed their old feathers to make way for new ones.

Species *is a group of similar animals.*

Nests

Birds lay eggs in nests that are built out of all kinds of things.

Handy tip

If you find a bird's nest, you should never disturb it.

Nimble nesters

If you look in your garden or up at the roof of your house, you may spot birds nesting there.

Super sparrows

Sparrows are common birds that chirp and cheep.

Pale streak near eye

One white bar

Black cheek patch

Two white bars

House sparrow

House sparrows nest in empty buildings and birdhouses. They can make their nest from paper, straw or even string.

Look for

A small light brown bird that has one white bar on each wing (female house sparrow). The male is grey and brown.

Tree sparrow

Tree sparrows may nest in trees or open woodland. Often, tree sparrows re-use the same nest year after year.

Look for

A small bird that has two white bars on each wing and a small black cheek patch.

Fascinating finches

Female goldfinches build nests on tree branches.

yellow wing streak

short tail

Look for

A black and white head, red face, yellow wing streak and a short tail. American goldfinches can be bright yellow!

Sticker activity
Find out the correct colours of an American goldfinch. Colour in your sticker and stick it in this box.

Nest cake recipe

Make edible nests by following this simple recipe.

chocolate eggs

chocolate covered shredded wheat

You'll need:

200g milk chocolate, broken into pieces
85g shredded wheat, crushed
2 × 100g bags mini chocolate eggs
12 cupcake cases

1. Ask an adult to melt the chocolate. Pour the chocolate over the shredded wheat and stir to combine.

2. Spoon the mixture into 12 cupcake cases and press a teaspoon in the centre of each to create a nest shape.

3. Chill the nests in the fridge until set, then decorate with chocolate eggs.

9

Pretty pigeons

Woodpigeons are very clever birds.

They build **platform nests** in trees. It takes months for them to make these nests, building them branch by branch.

Look for

A grey body, white neck patch and white wing patches.

white neck patch

white wing patch

*A **platform nest** is a large nest usually found up in a tree.*

Feathering the nest

Colour in your egg and feather stickers and fill the nest with them.

Soaring Songbirds

Sticker activity
Use your bird stickers to complete this scene.

Handy tip
Sometimes you can hear birds close by, even if you can't see them.

A selection of songs

Not all birds can sing, but some can make lots of different songs.

Collecting bird sounds

You can "collect" bird sounds by listening to songbirds and noting down what their songs sound like.

Activity

How many sounds can you collect? Can you find out which bird the song belongs to?

Singing starlings

Starlings are common garden singers.

A flock of starlings is called a murmuration, which is when thousands of starlings swoop and dive together in the sky.

Look for

A sleek black bird with a short, squared tail.

short tail

Fun fact

Starlings are able to copy many different sounds.

Swallows and martins

Swallows and martins have a twittering song.

They also have calls for speaking to other birds.

Fun fact
During the winter, swallows can travel hundreds of miles a day in search of warm weather.

blue feathers

blue back

forked tail

long forked tail

Look for

A dark blue back and a short forked tail (martin).

Look for

Blue feathers, a red throat, a long forked tail and a white belly (swallow).

A chirp-along!

Colour in your musical note stickers and stick them on the scale below to make your own bird song. Can you play the song on a simple recorder?

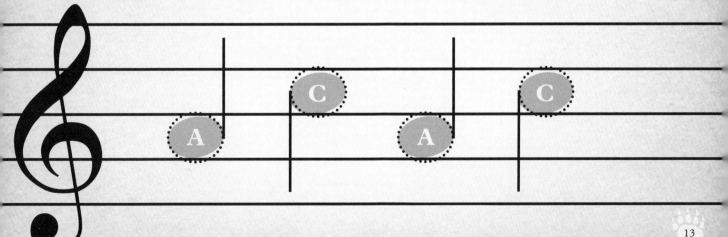

13

The thrush family

Thrushes sing amazing songs.

Blackbirds and robins are part of the thrush family.
They have short beaks and long legs.

Bold blackbirds

The blackbird's song sounds a bit like a flute.

You may hear it in the morning or evening.

Look for

Black feathers and a bright orange-yellow beak (male blackbird) or brown feathers (female blackbird).

Fun fact

Blackbirds have strong beaks for pulling out bugs hidden in the soil.

Activity

Blackbirds love eating worms. Can you spot ten worms hidden on these pages?

bright beak

black feathers

Rockin' robin

Robins sing all year round.

They have a bright red breast. American robins have an orange breast.

Joke corner

What is a robin?
A bird who steals!

Handprint robin

Ask an adult to help you make a robin. It works best with two different-sized hands!

You'll need:

Red poster or washable paint
Brown poster or washable paint
A black pen
PVA glue, paper and scissors

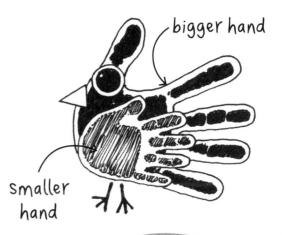

bigger hand

smaller hand

1. Bigger hand: keep all your fingers together and print a brown handprint on the centre of a piece of paper.

2. Smaller hand: print a red handprint onto another piece of paper and let it dry.

3. Cut out the red handprint and glue it to the brown print.

4. Draw on wings, eyes, legs and a beak.

Sticker activity

Find out the correct colours of an American robin. Colour in your sticker and stick it in this box.

red breast

Larking about

Skylarks are famous for their song.

They are one of the first birds you may hear in the morning. Skylarks have a small crest that is not always visible.

crest

Look for

A pale brown bird with a short tail and a strong pointed bill.

Fun fact
A group of larks can be called an exaltation.

Splashing about

Make a fun place for songbirds to bathe. Once you're done, wait to see who visits the bird bath.

You'll need:

Terracotta pot and saucer
Poster paint and paintbrush
Paper plate for the paint
Bird bath colour-in stickers

terracotta saucer

stickers

terracotta pot

1. Find a place in your garden to position the bird bath.

2. Paint the pot and saucer any colour you like – the brighter the better – and leave to dry.

3. Colour in your bird stickers and decorate the pot and saucer.

4. Turn the pot upside down, place the saucer on top and fill it with water.

Water Dwellers

Sticker activity

Use your bird stickers to fill in this scene.

Fun fact

Swans can sleep on water as well as land.

Wonderful waterfowl

Some birds have feathers and feet that make it easier for them to live on water.

Stately swans

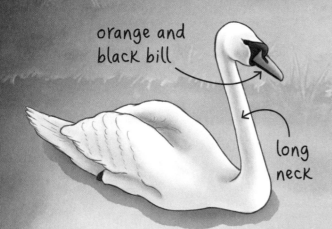

orange and black bill

long neck

Mute swans look very elegant gliding on the water.

They are large white birds that can also fly. Mute swans have a long neck and an orange and black bill.

A graceful game

Make your own swan from a paper plate.

You'll need:

One paper plate
Pencil and scissors
Beak and eye stickers
Colour-in feather stickers

1. Draw the dotted line in the picture on the paper plate. Ask an adult to help cut along the dotted line.

2. Add feathers, an eye and a beak using your stickers.

Can you make a game of swans?

Fun fact
A group of swans is known as a "game".

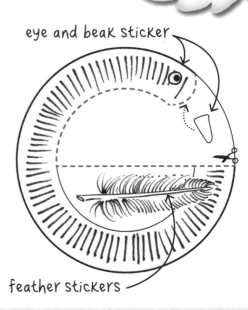

eye and beak sticker

feather stickers

white throat patch

Gaggling geese

Canada geese can be spotted flying in a V **formation**. A flock of geese in flight is called a skein.

Look for

A black head and neck and white throat patch. Baby Canada geese are yellow and fluffy.

Fun fact
The sound a goose makes is called a "honk".

Formation *is the shape formed by birds in flight.*

Brilliant kingfishers

Kingfishers are colourful birds that hover over water as they search for fish.

Look for

A blue and orange head, short orange legs and blue-green wings. Female American belted kingfishers have a red band across their belly.

small white bib

Sticker activity
Find out the correct colours of an American belted kingfisher. Colour in your sticker and stick it in this box.

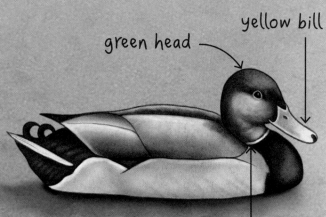

green head

yellow bill

white neckband

Downy ducks

Mallards have shorter necks and wings than swans and geese.

The male mallard is an easy duck to spot, as it is brightly coloured.

Look for

A green head, a long yellow bill and white neckband (male mallard). Female mallards have a brown body and an orange bill.

Fun fact

A group of ducks can be called a flock, a brace or team.

Get your ducks in a row!

Colour in your duck stickers and use them to play this simple game of three in a row. First one to get their ducks in a row wins!

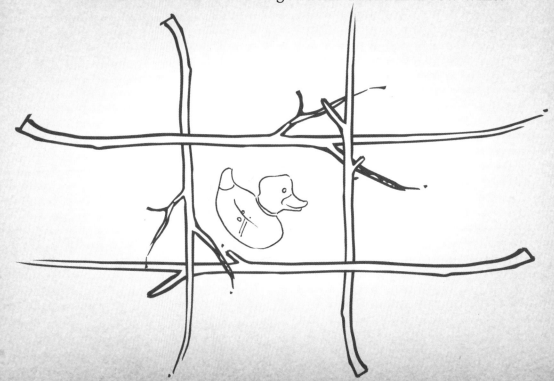

Birds of Prey

Fun fact
Owls are known for their hoot but they can also chirp and shriek.

Sticker activity
Use your bird stickers to complete this scene.

Beady-eyed birds

Birds of prey feed on small mammals.

These birds have good eyesight, hearing and curved claws that help them to catch their food.

A *mammal* is a warm-blooded animal that has a backbone.

long wings

white face

Barn owls have eyes that are like binoculars.

They can see far-away things very clearly, but they can't see very well up close.

Look for

A white face, dark eyes and long wings.

Birdwatching binoculars

Find birds with a pair of binoculars! Follow these simple instructions and see what you can spot.

You'll need:

String, tape, 2 toilet rolls
Scissors, hole punch, coloured paper
Stickers to decorate

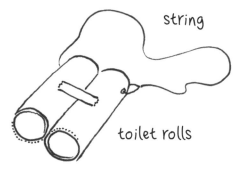

string

toilet rolls

1. Ask an adult to help cover two toilet rolls with coloured paper.

2. Line up the covered tubes side by side and stick them together with two pieces of tape, one at the top and one at the bottom.

3. Make a hole in the outside edge of each tube with a hole punch.

4. Cut a length of string for your neck strap. Thread each end through the hole on either side, then tie a knot.

5. Use your stickers to decorate your binoculars.

Regal eagles

Golden eagles are large birds of prey.

They can spot prey from very high up in the air.

Look for

A large brown bird with golden feathers on the back of its neck.

large wings

golden feathers

Sticker activity
Draw these birds of prey in a journal and use your beak and eye stickers to add details.

talons

Fast falcons

Peregrine falcons are medium-sized birds of prey.

They are some of the fastest birds in the world and capture prey with their sharp talons.

Look for

Long, pointed wings, a blue-grey coat and a black mark on its face.

Calling crows

Ravens and rooks are part of the crow family.

Ravens are large birds that make a deep "croak" sound.

Look for

Black feathers, a big bill and long wings.

Rooks are usually seen in flocks. They make a call that sounds like "kaah".

Look for

Black feathers with a purplish gloss.

Sticker activity

Colour in your speech bubble stickers and stick them here to match the call to the crow. Can you match your extra stickers to the calls on pages 19 and 27?

Joke corner

How do crows stick together in a flock? **Velcrow.**

Seashore Sightings

Sticker activity 🐾
Complete this seaside scene
using your bird stickers.

Fun fact
A group of gulls can
be called a colony.

Seaside visitors

There are some amazing birds that visit the seashore.

Gulls are small seabirds. Their long, slim wings help them fly and their strong legs make them steady on the ground. They often rest on water.

Herring gulls

You can see herring gulls at the coast, near playing fields and where rubbish is collected – as they eat whatever they can find.

Look for

Light grey back, black wing tips and pink legs.

black wing tips

pink legs

Handy tip

You may spot seaside birds in the towns and cities nearby.

Wonderful waders

Curlews are part of the sandpiper family of birds.

They are large wading birds that can be recognized by their call that sounds like "twee-wee" as they fly away.

Look for

A downturned bill, brown feathers and long legs.

Activity

Have you spotted any bird prints on your adventure? Can you find out who they belong to?

downturned bill

brown feathers

Sticker activity

Colour in your footprint stickers and stick them along the dotted line.

yellow bill

black legs

Crafty kittiwakes

Kittiwakes can be spotted nesting on cliff ledges.

They make their nests from things like mud and feathers.

Look for

A medium-sized bird with a small yellow bill, grey back and short black legs.

Coastal craft activity

Next time you visit the seaside, why not make a picture in the sand of some of the birds you have seen?

You'll need:

Flat brown, grey and black rocks

1. Pick up any flat rocks when you're on the beach.

2. Sort the rocks into groups of colours.

3. Use one group of rocks to make an outline in the shape of a bird in the sand.

4. Use different colour rocks to add details like an eye, beak, wings and feet.

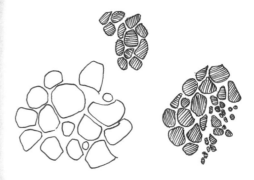

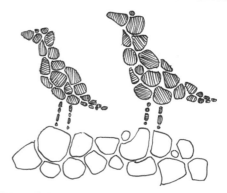

Take a picture of your creation so that you can look at it once you get home.

Perfect puffins

If you're really lucky, you might spot a puffin!

They can be seen near the coast and in special puffin **colonies**. Sadly the number of puffins is decreasing.

Look for

A black coat, white cheeks, bright orange legs and a multi-coloured bill.

bright bill

white cheeks

black coat

*A **colony** is a group of animals living together in the same space.*

Activity

Turn to page 32 to find out how you can help our feathered friends.

Can you spot four differences between these scenes?

Spotter's list

Put a sticker next to any birds you have seen on your bird search. Some of the stickers can be coloured in!

Woodpigeon

Goldfinch

Birds Close to Home

Tree sparrow

House sparrow

Soaring Songbirds

Swall[ow]

Martin

Blackbird

Starling

Skylark

Robin

Water Dwellers

Kingfisher

Canada goose

Mute swan

Mallard

Rook

Golden eagle

Birds of Prey

Peregrine falcon

Raven

Barn owl

Fun fact
A cup nest is a common type of nest that is bowl-shaped.

H

Seashore Sightings

Kittiwake

Curlew

Puffi

Help your feathered friends

Birds make our world a more beautiful place to live.

There is plenty we can do to help keep birds safe and happy.

Making a bird feeder is a great way to provide food for birds and to encourage them to nest nearby.

Feed the birds

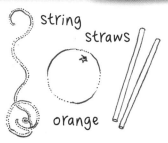

Ask an adult to help you make a homemade bird feeder. Once you've hung it in your garden, wait and see who visits!

You'll need:

1 large orange	2 straws
String	Bird seed
A spoon	Scissors

1. Ask an adult to cut the orange in half. Use the spoon to remove the fruit from inside the orange peel so you are left with a cup.

2. Poke both straws through the orange, criss-crossing them in the middle.

3. Cut two equal-sized pieces of string (approximately half a metre long).

4. Tie each end of the string to each side of the straws.

5. Fill with bird seed and hang the bird feeder at the top of both pieces of string.

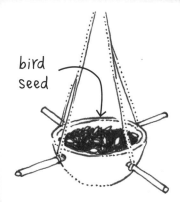

bird seed

Page 5.

© 2016 Bear Hunt Films Ltd

Bird stickers

Page 11.

Page 21.

Page 17.

Page 25.

Page 18.

Page 23.

Page 22.

Page 30/31.

CROAK!

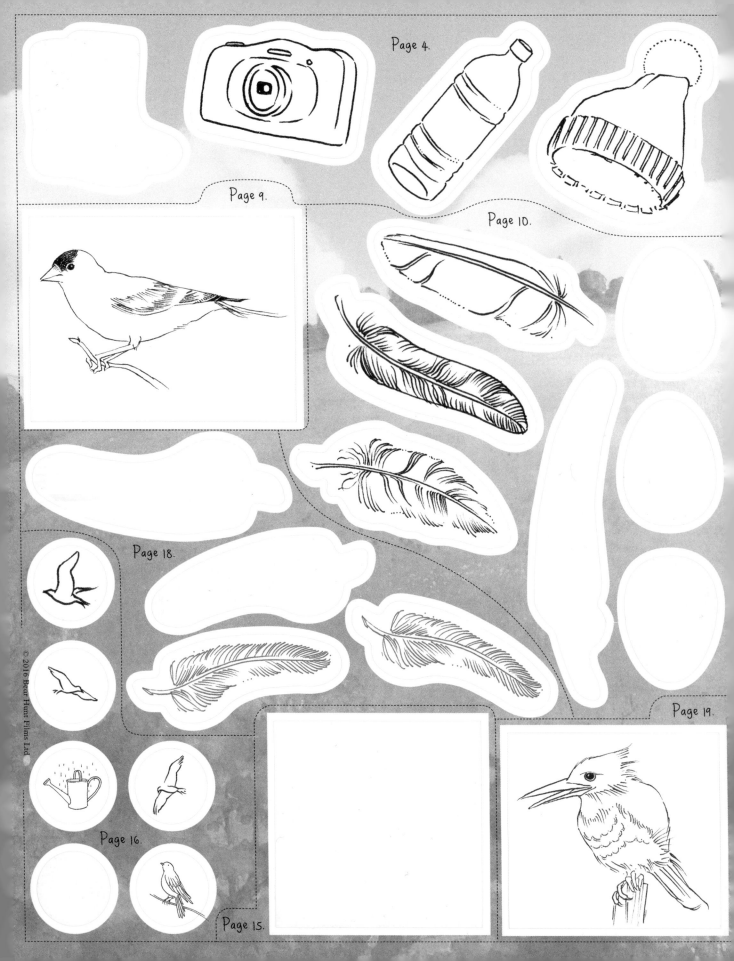

Page 4.

Page 9.

Page 10.

Page 18.

Page 19.

Page 16.

Page 15.

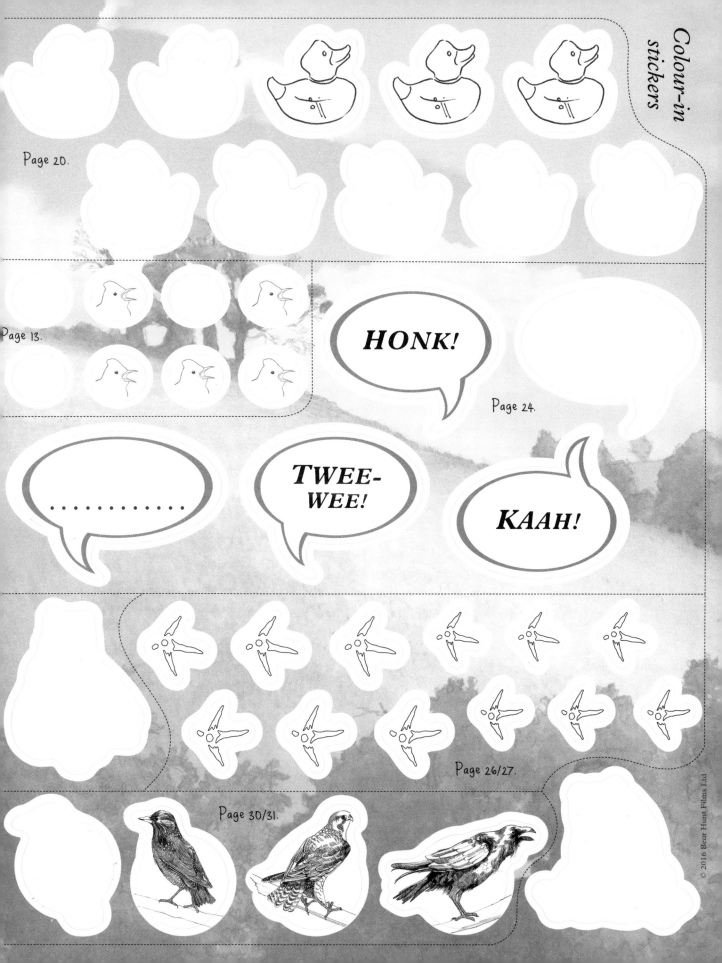